Dark Starlight Publications

Presents

Sunsets of the Soul- A book of Photography

By

Patti Sassy Angel Chiappa

Dark Starlight Publications

2605 Legend Ct

Leesburg, FL 34748

Ordering Information:

Quantity sales. Special discounts are available on quantity purchases by corporations, associations, and others. For details, contact the publisher at the address above.

Orders by U.S. trade bookstores and wholesalers. Contact: Soulbabylondon@gmail.com

Printed in the United States of America 2016

Eiffel Tower at Night- Paris France

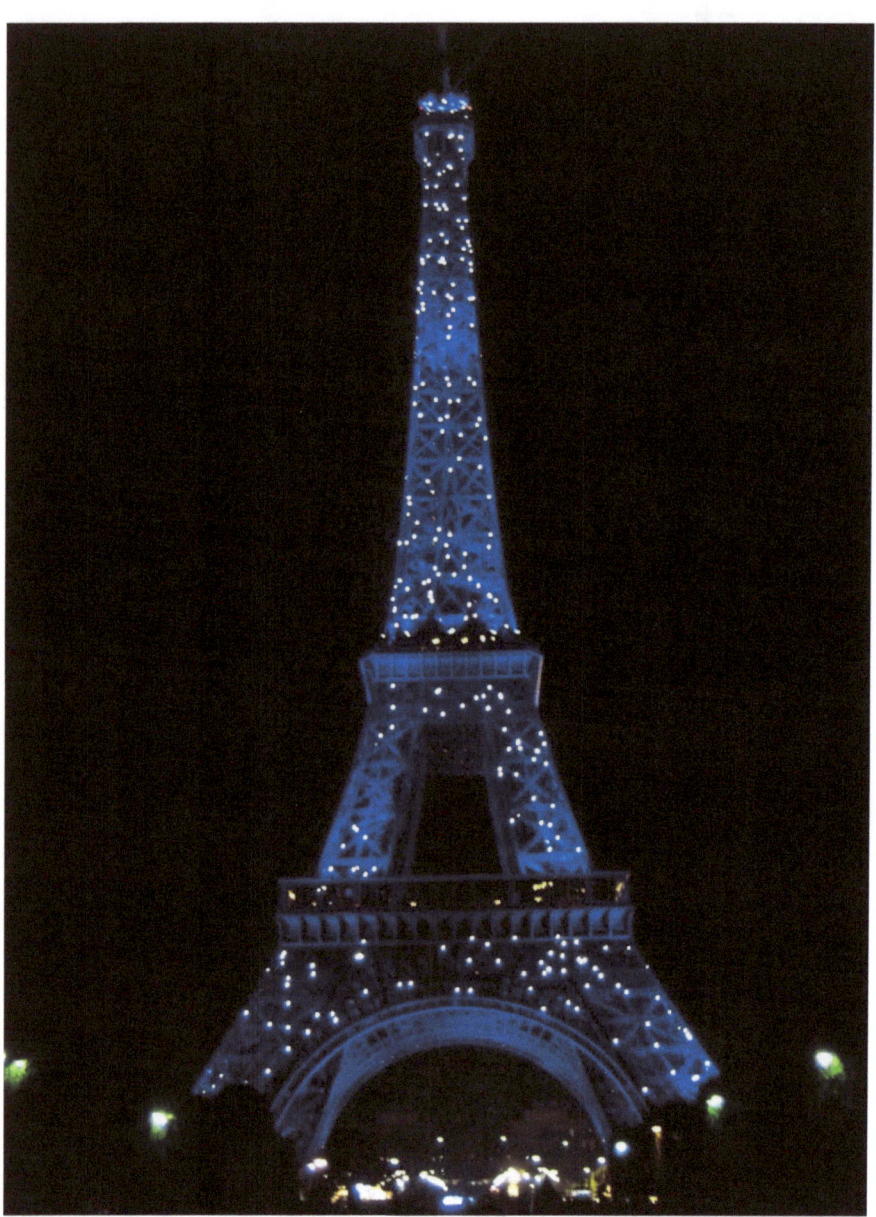

A China Garden

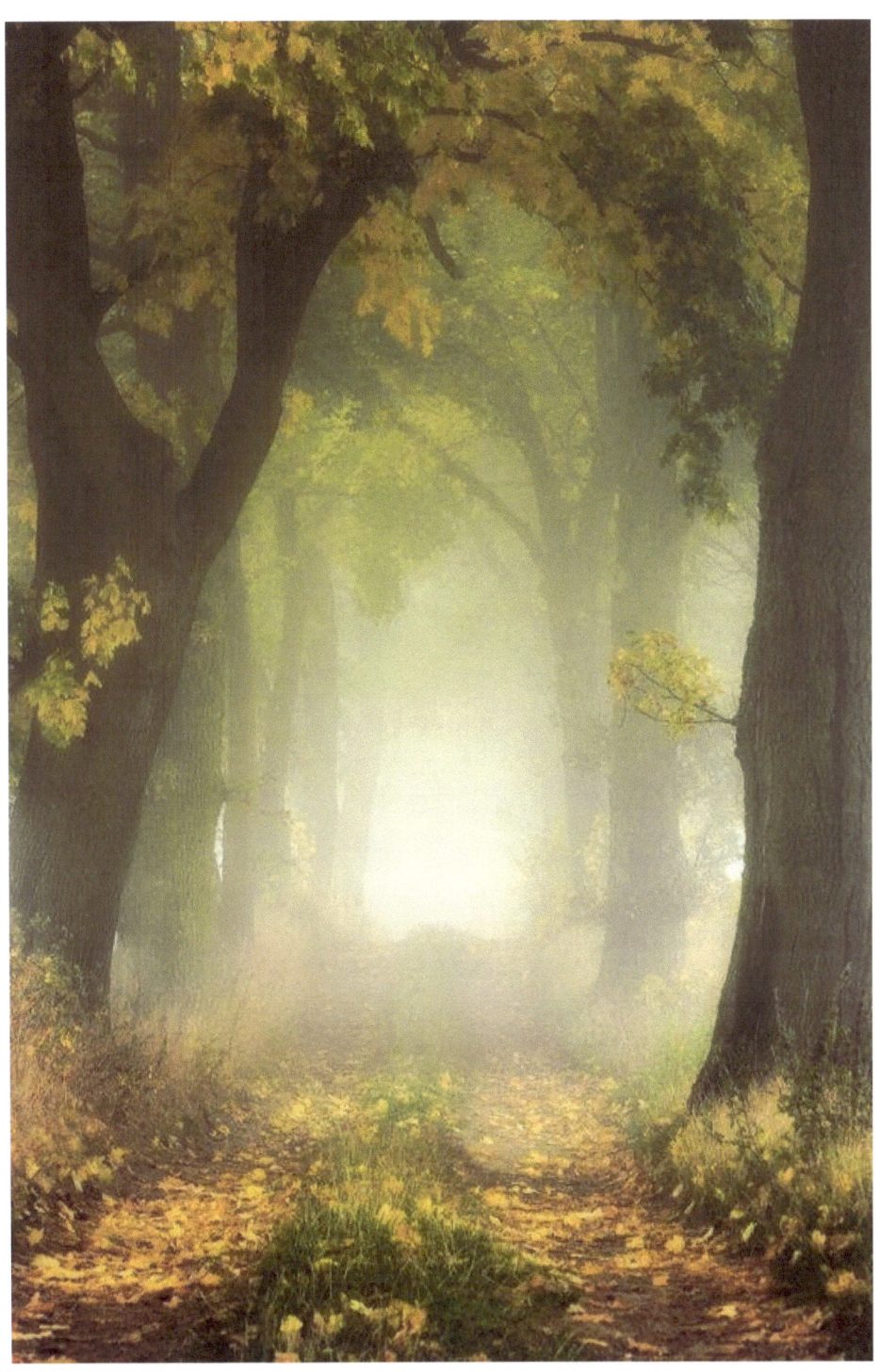

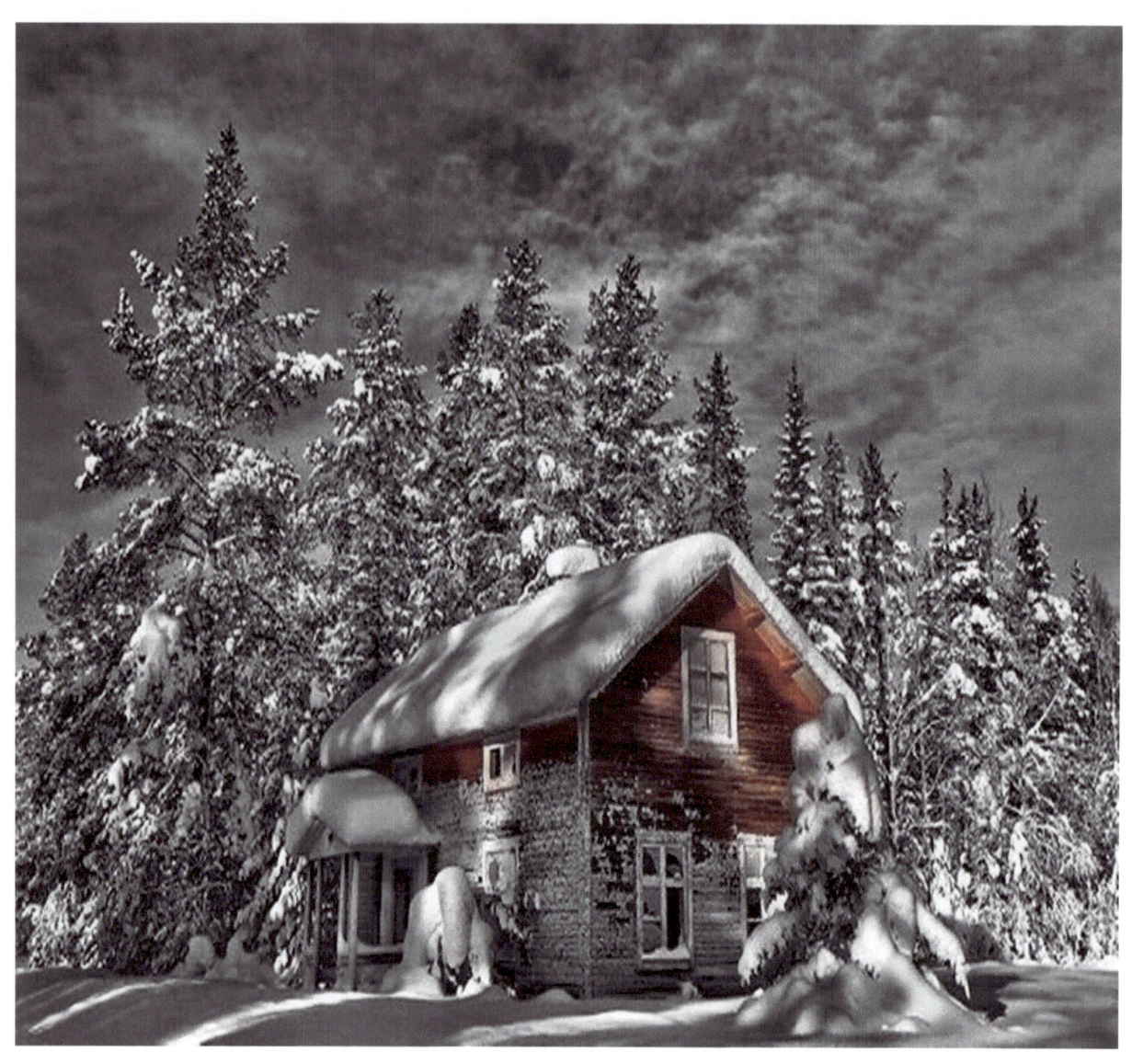

The Red Barn- Portland Maine

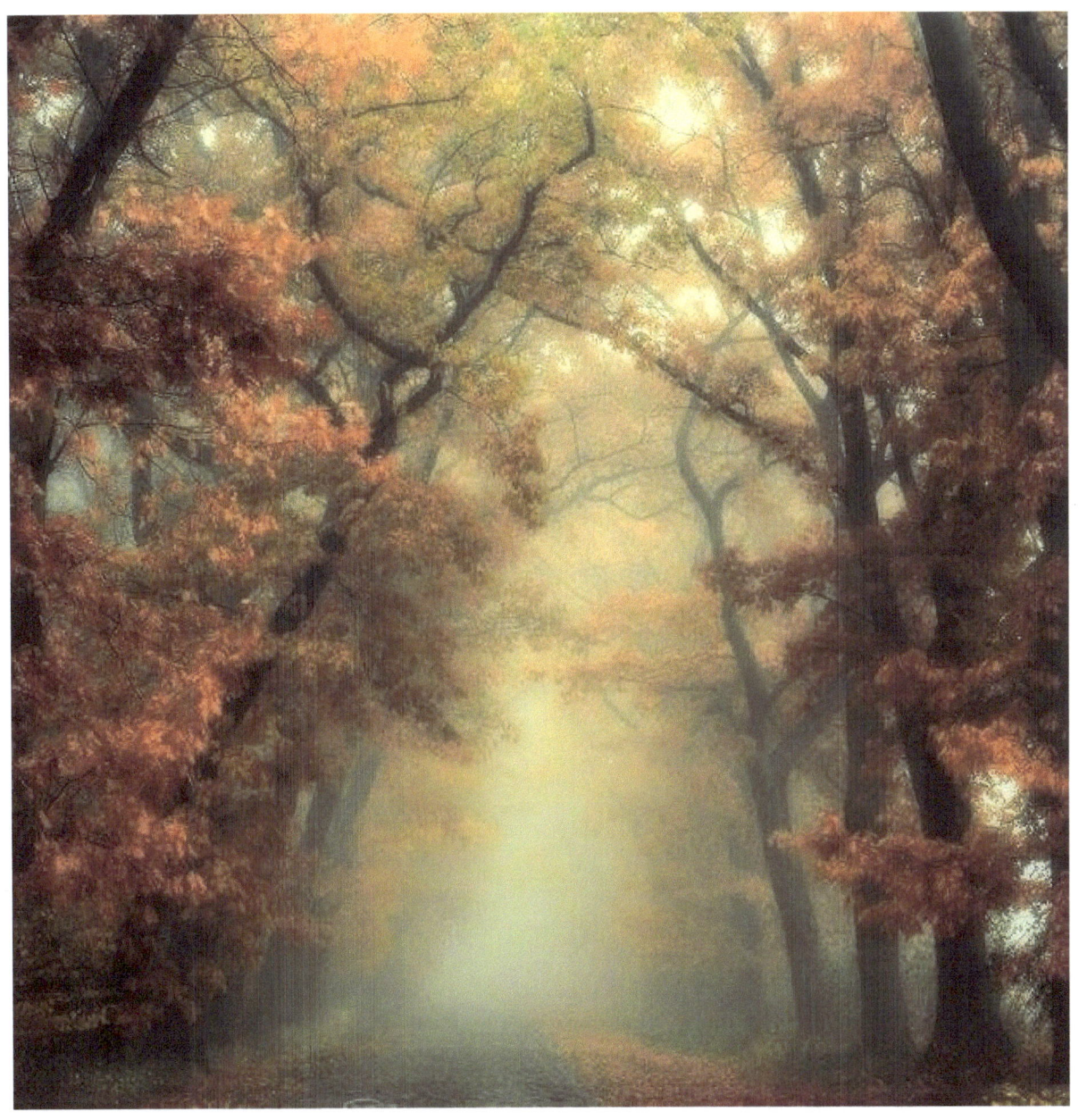

An Autumn Day in New York

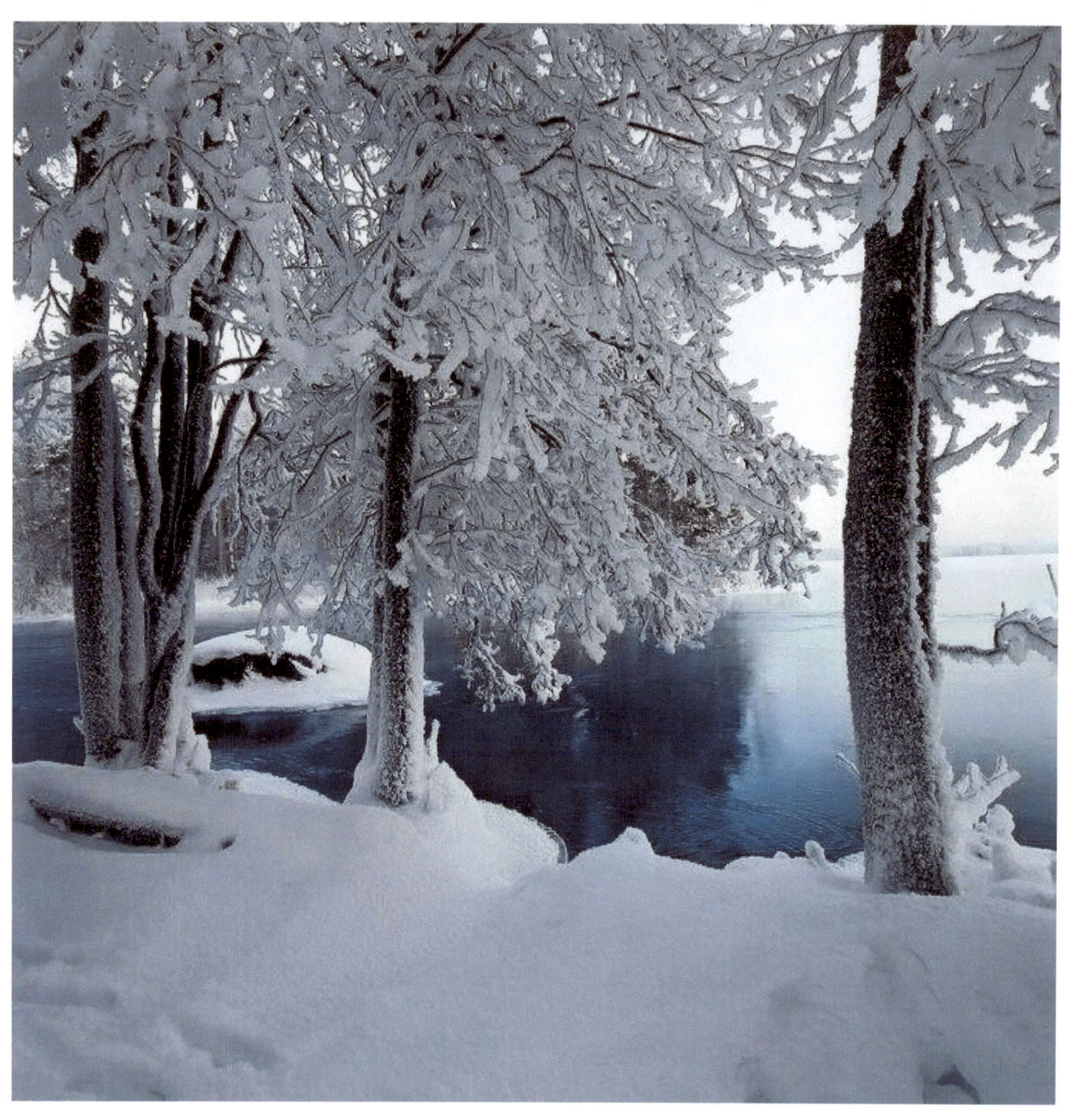

Snowy Afternoon in Denver , Colorado

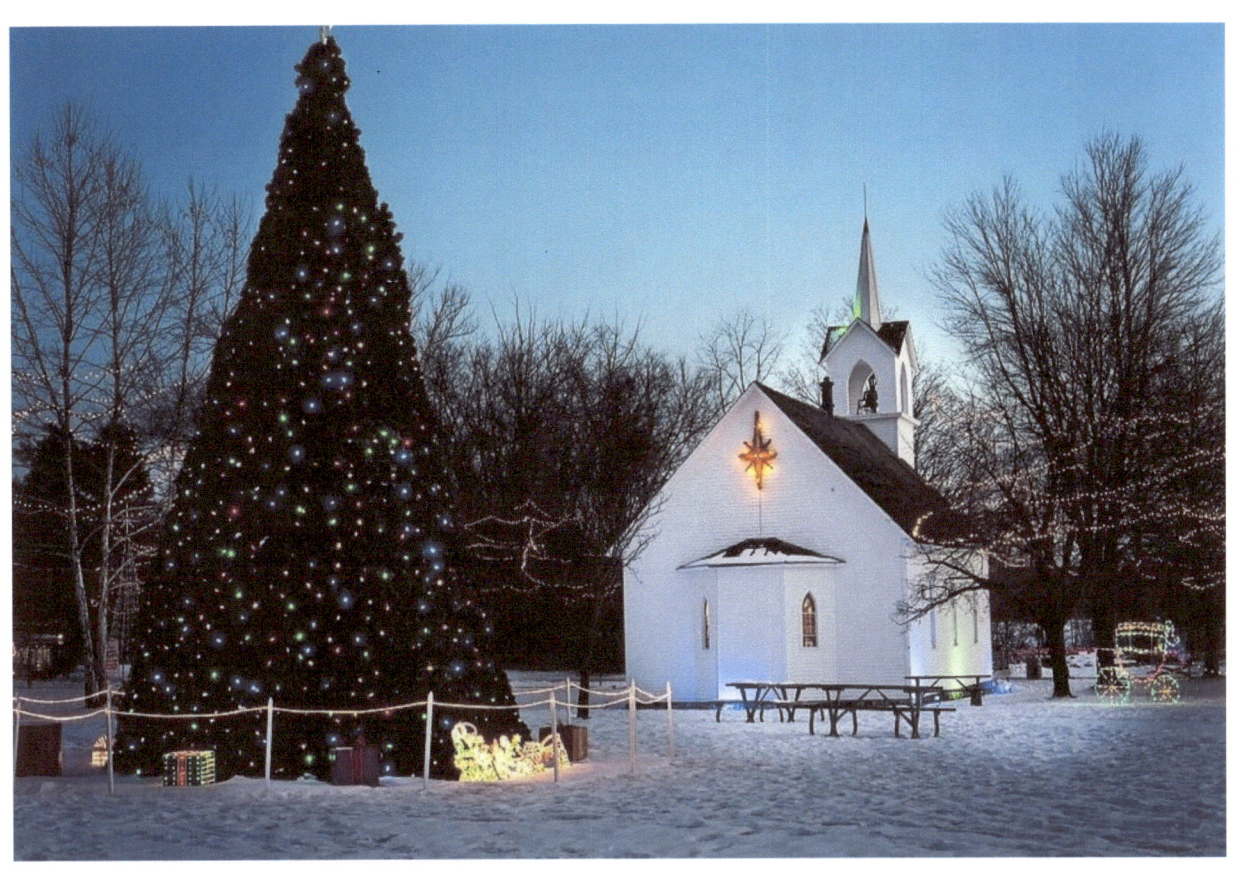

Peaceful Night- Long Island, New York

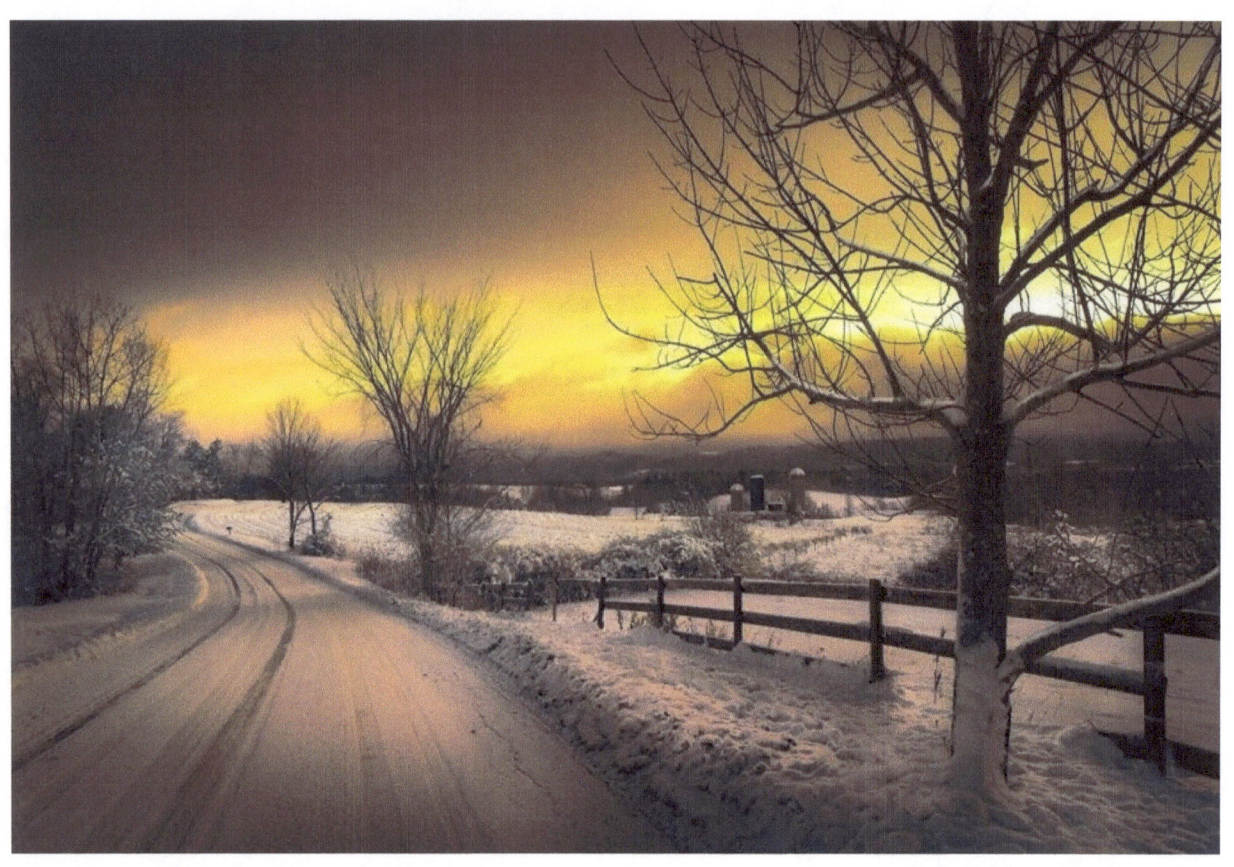

Winter Wonderland- Iceland

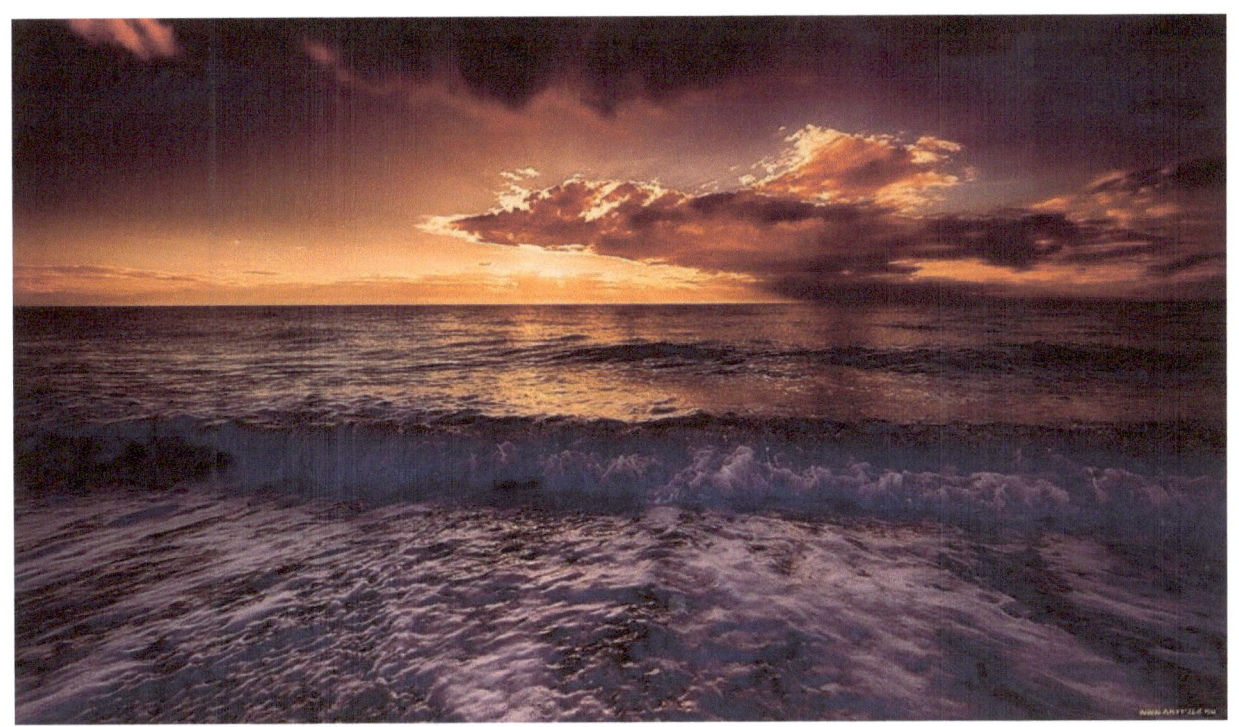

Beach Dreaming- Hawaii

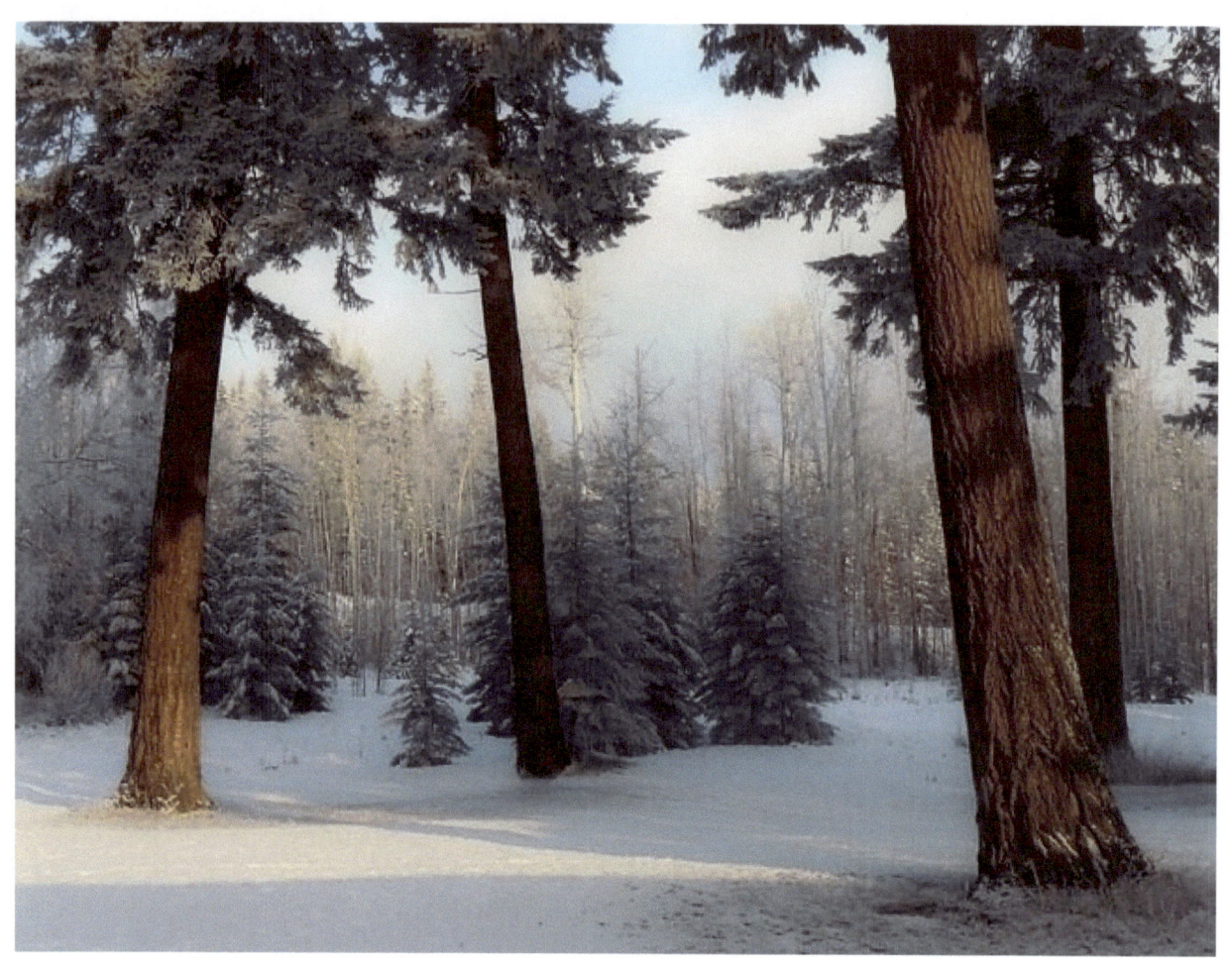

In the Pines- Massachusetts

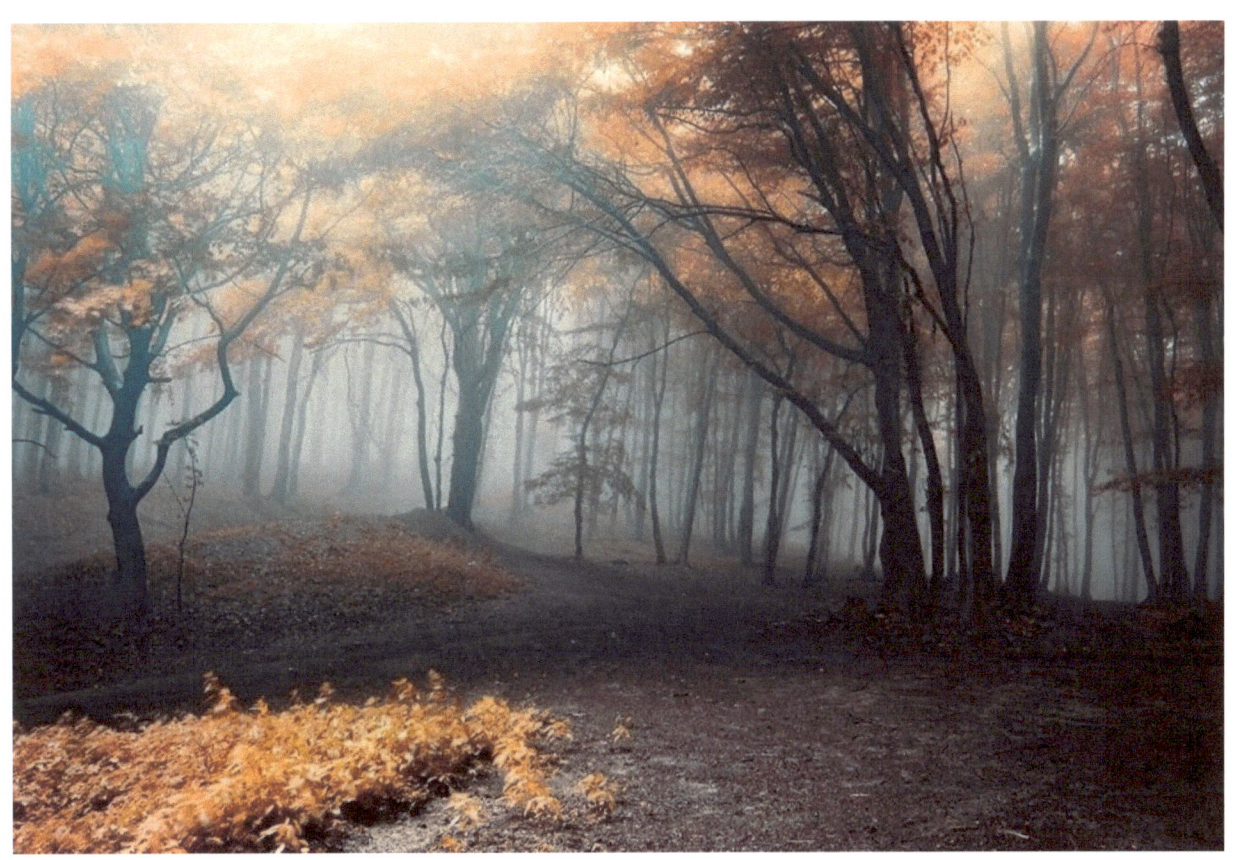

The road to nowhere- Scotland

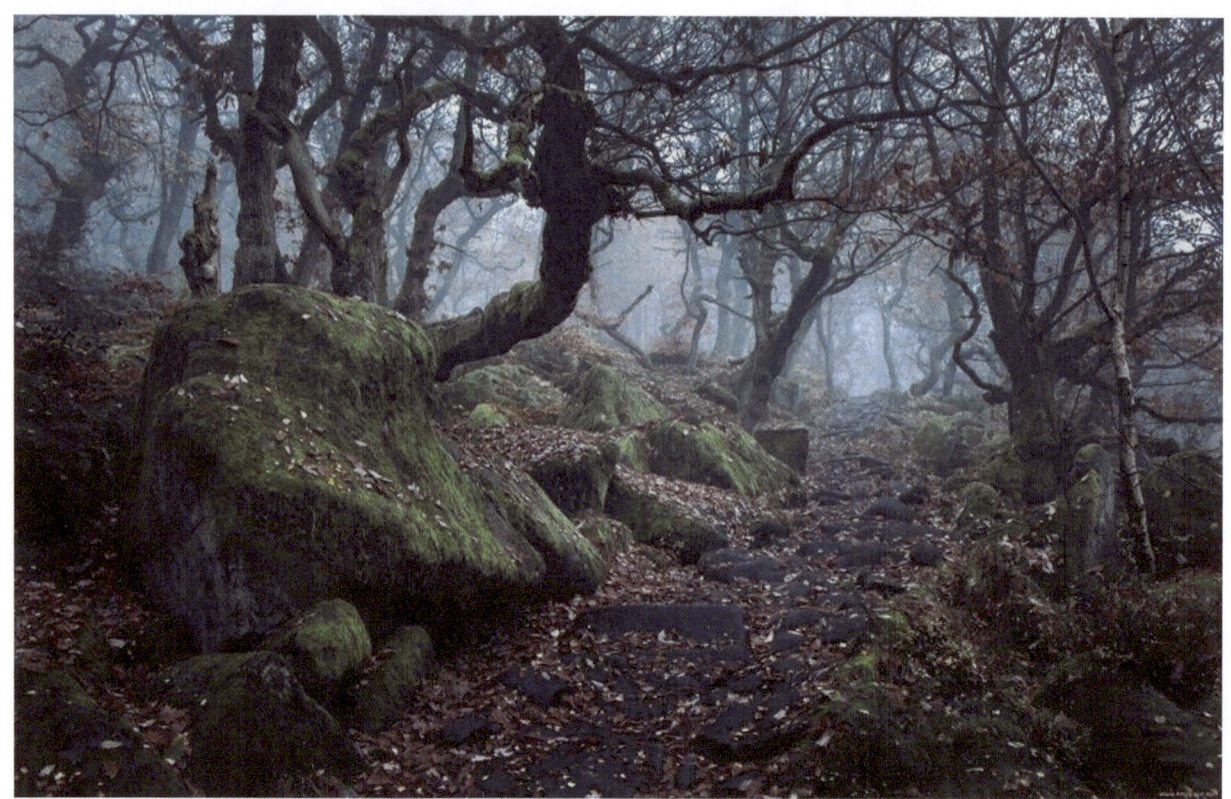

Ireland

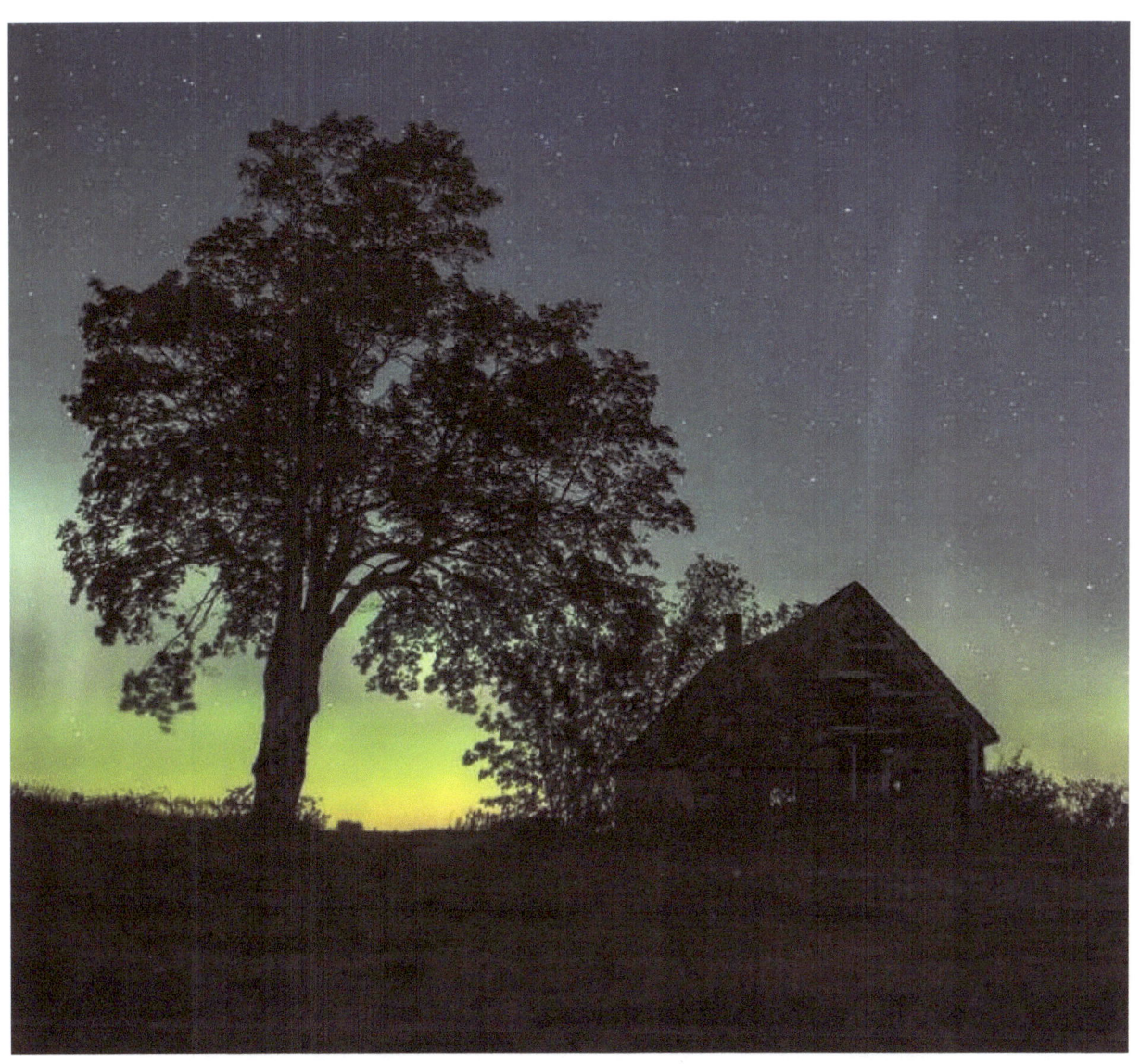

Stargazing in Poland

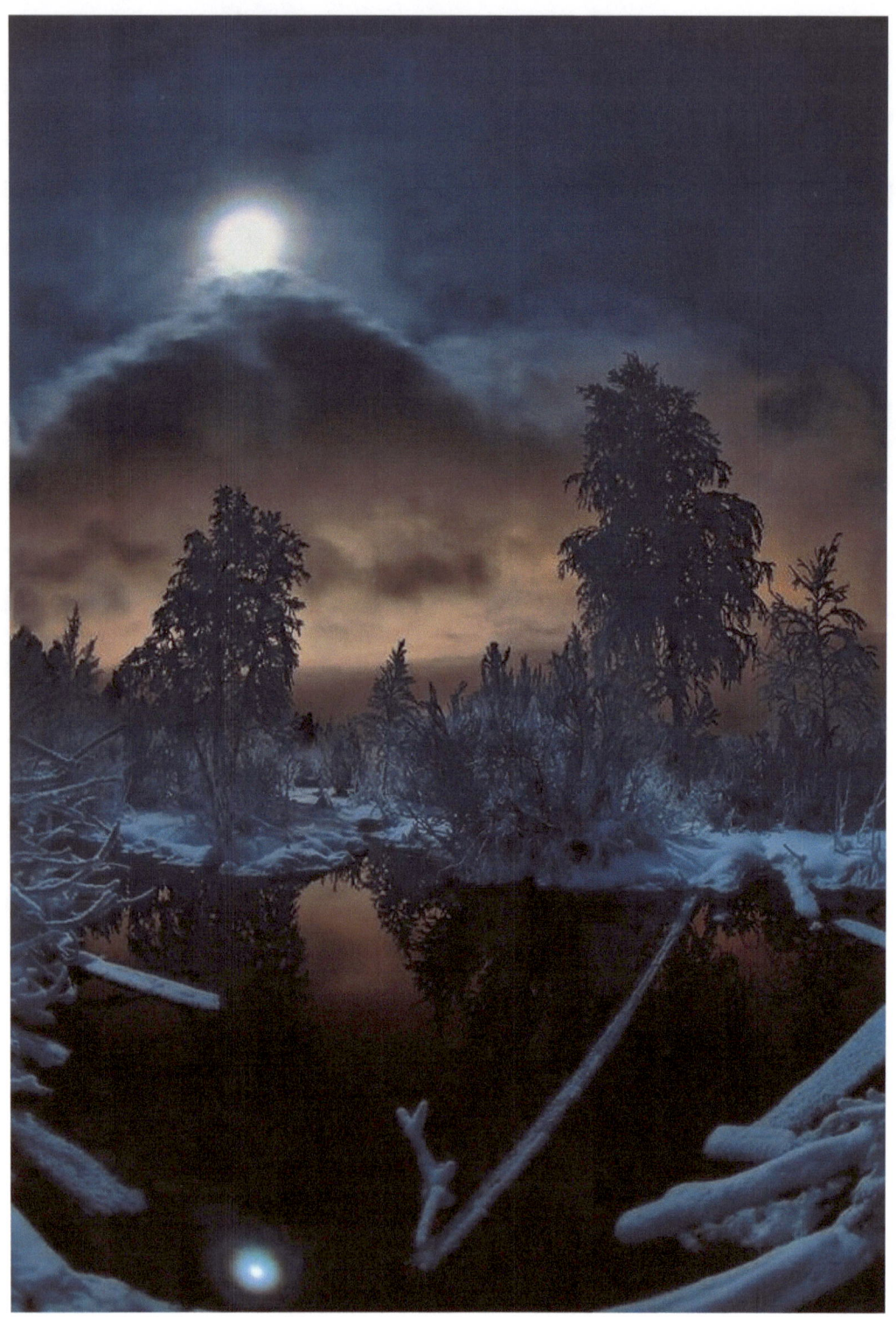

Moonlit night- Germany

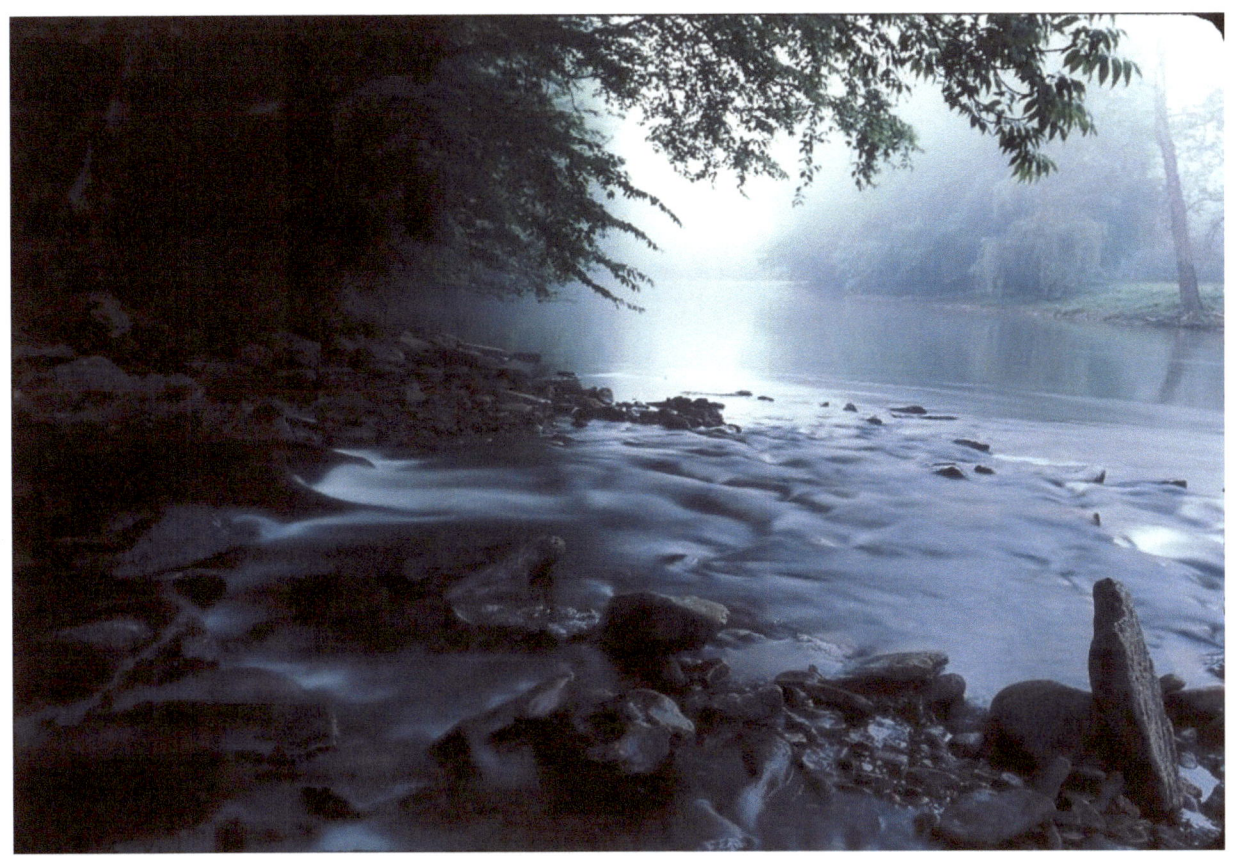

Healing Waters- Rome

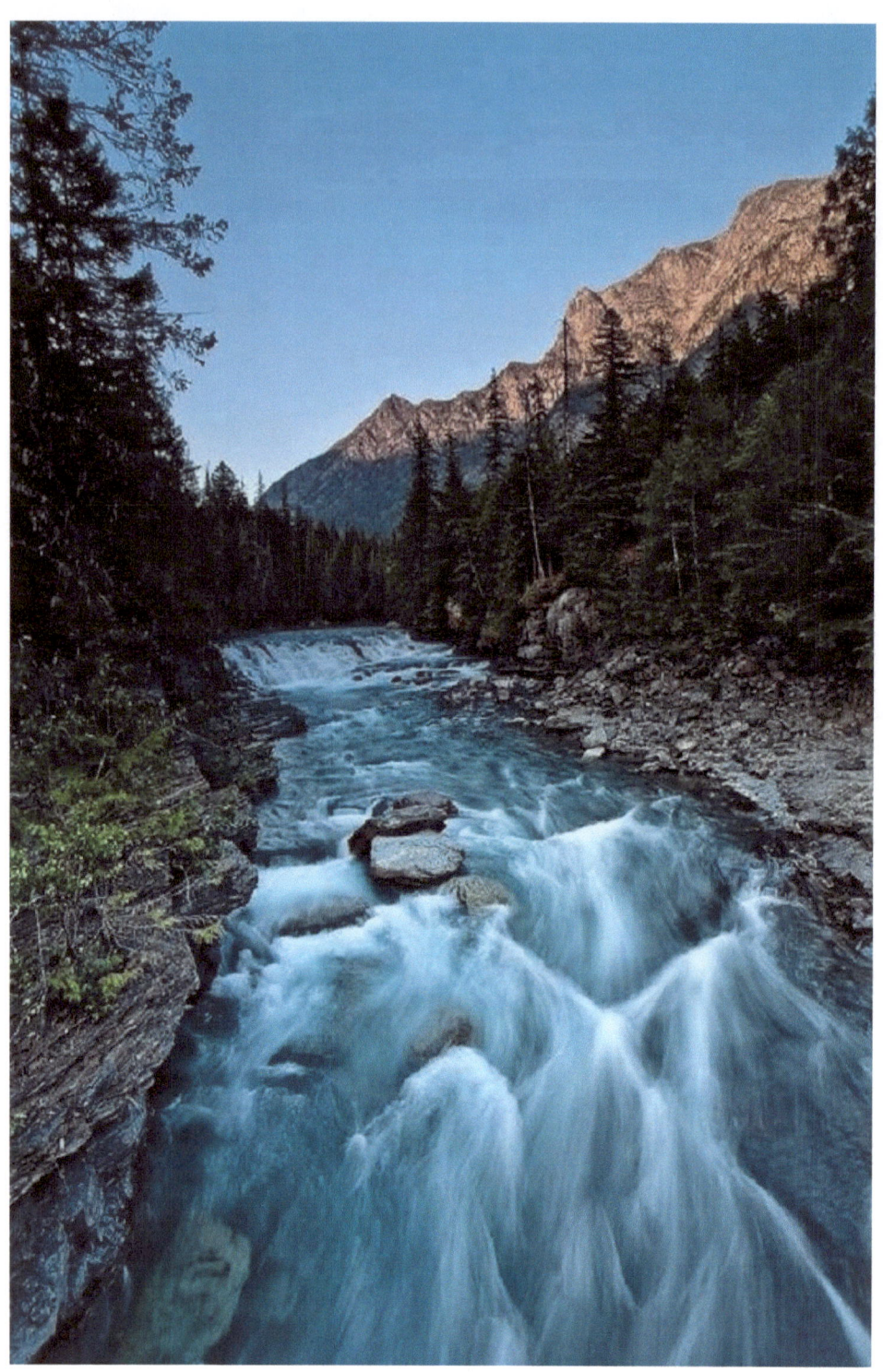

Peaceful Moment- New Jersey

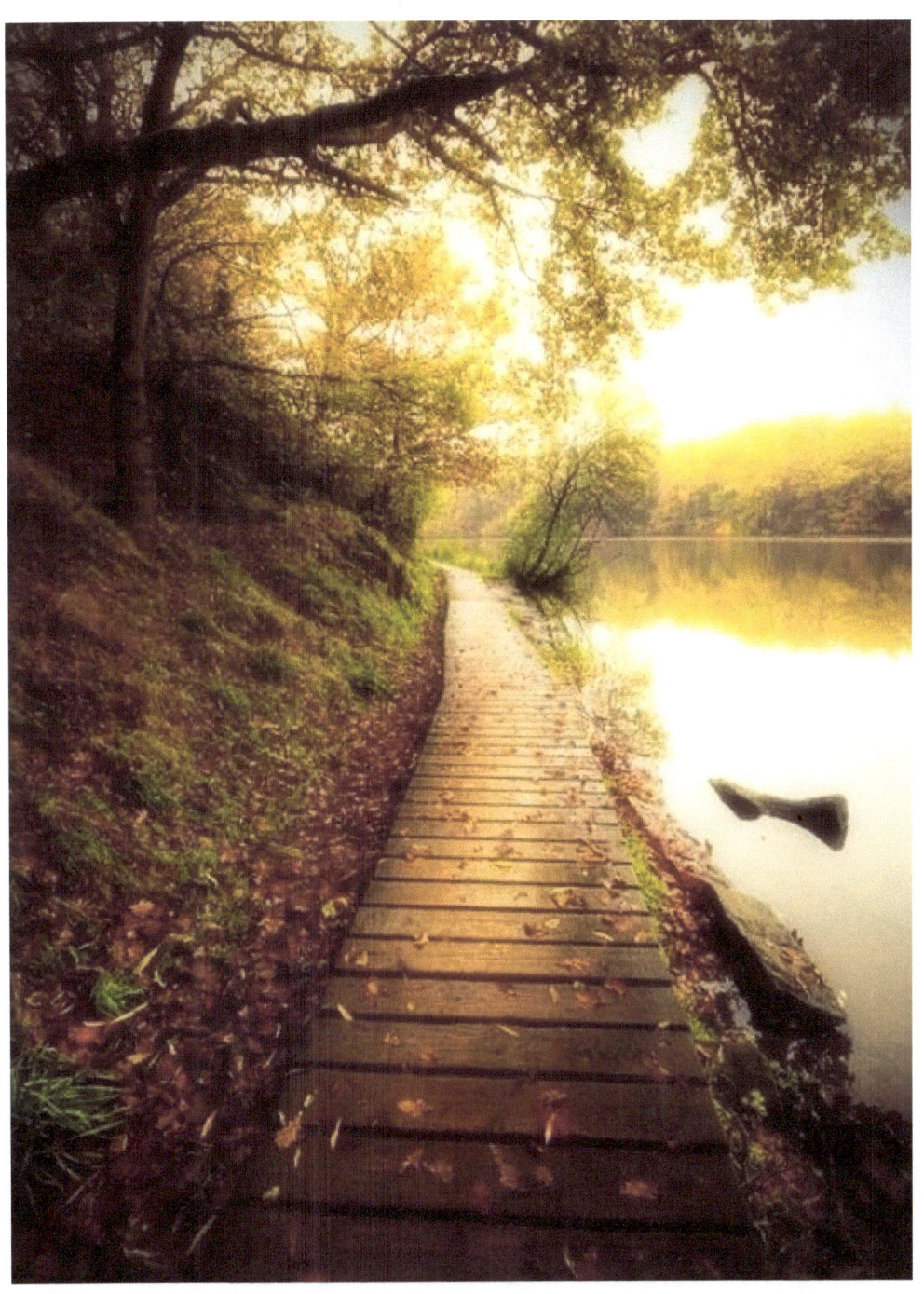

Thru God's eye- Summer in Covington, Georgia

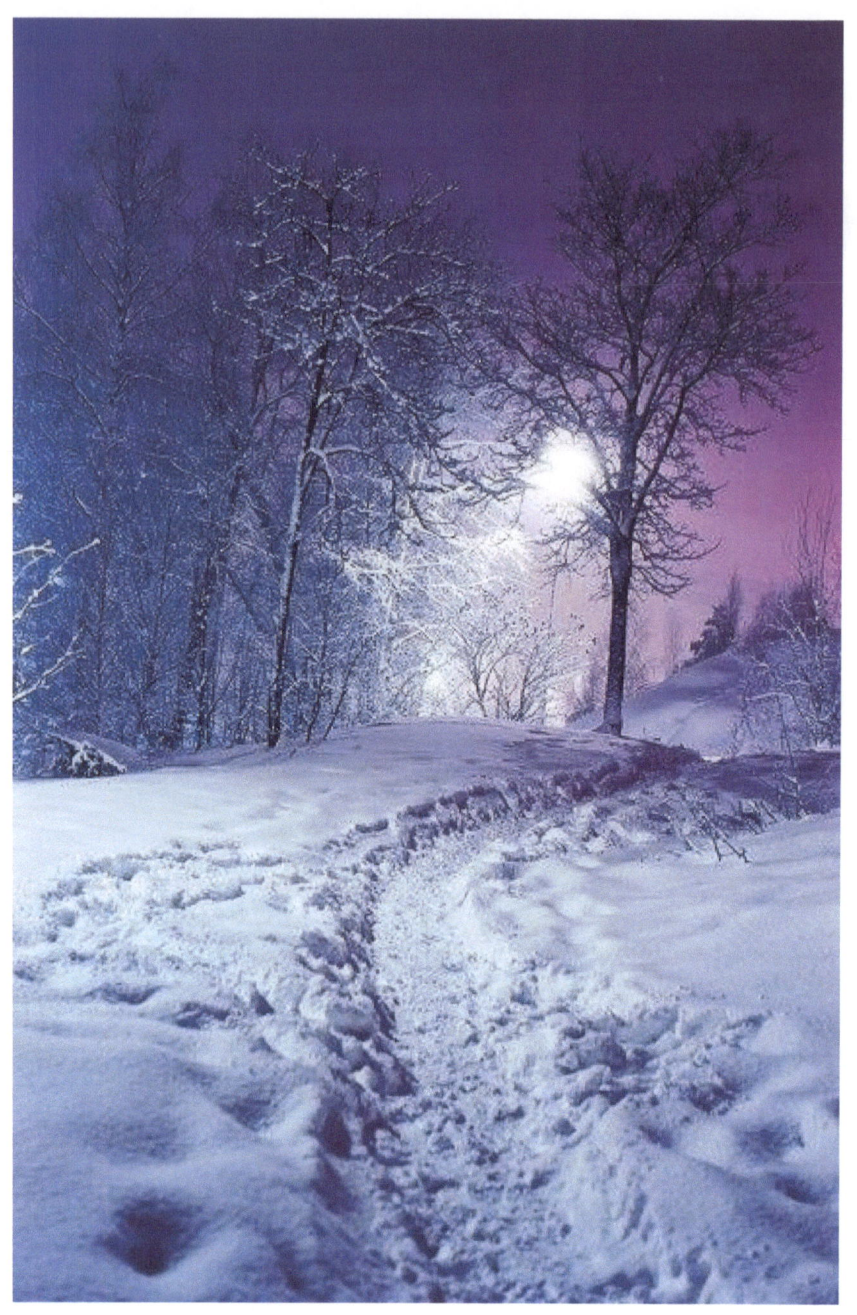

Dance with the Moon- North Carolina

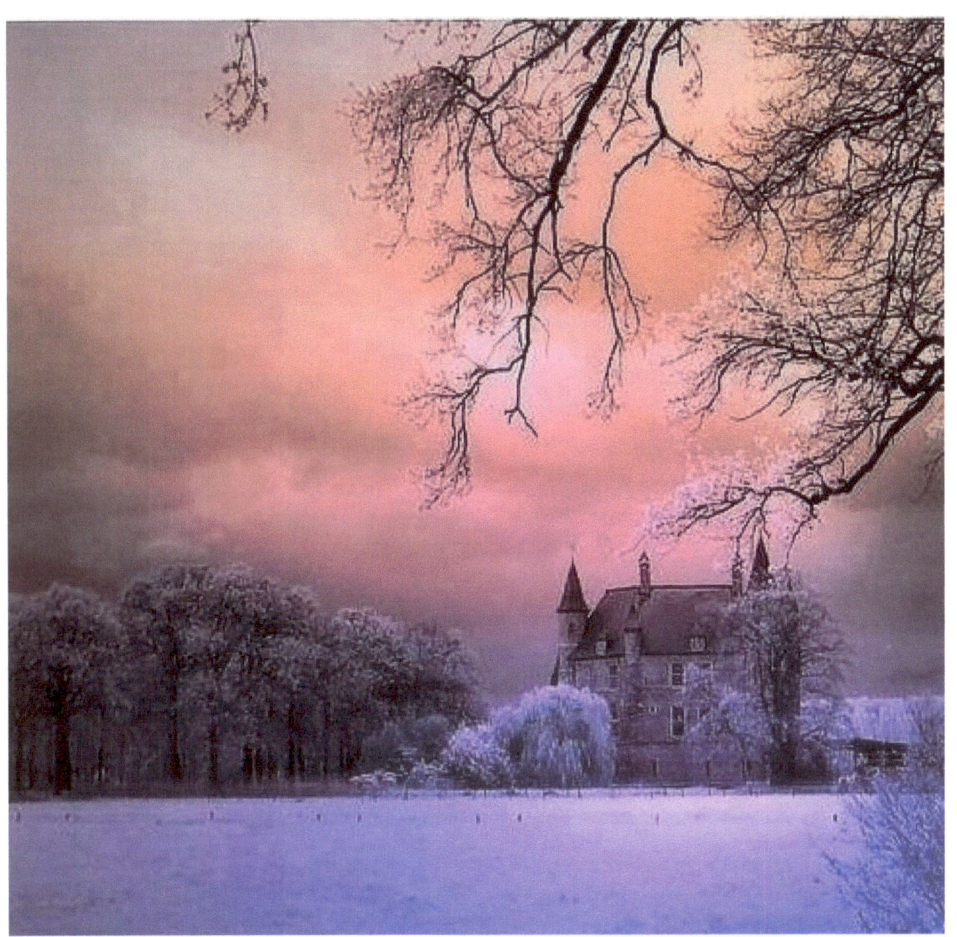

Pink Rapture- London

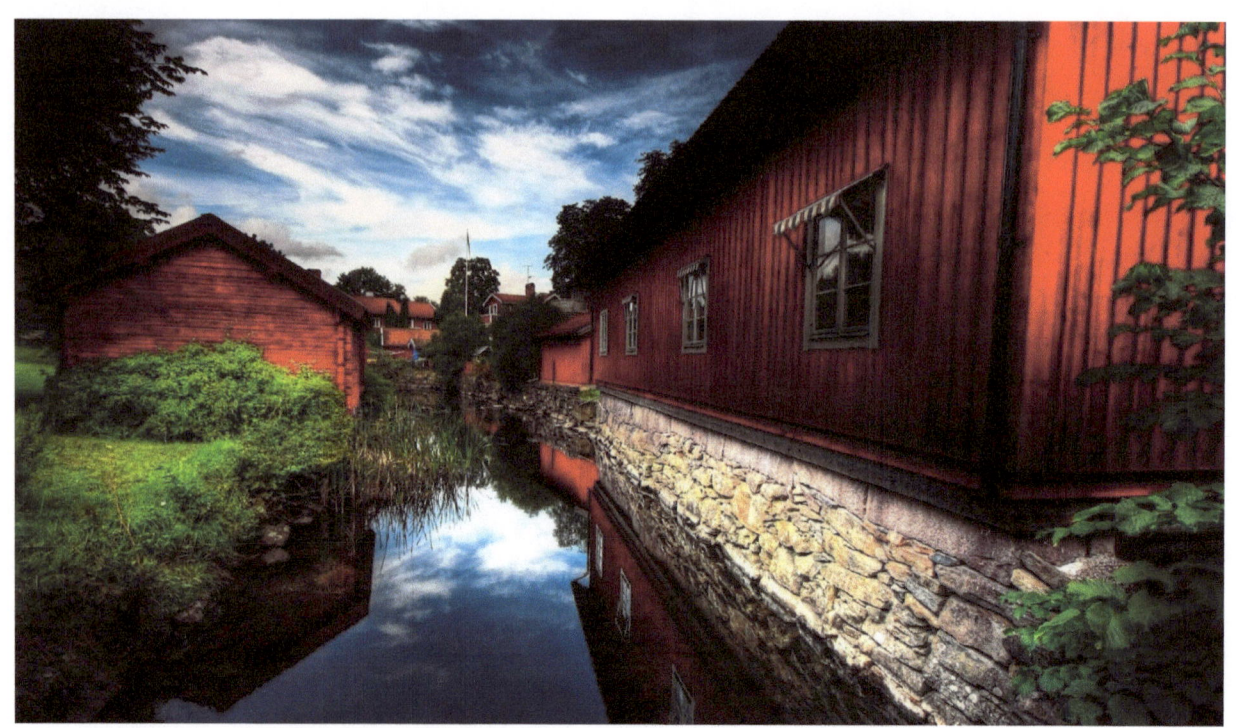

A view from down here- Long Island , New York

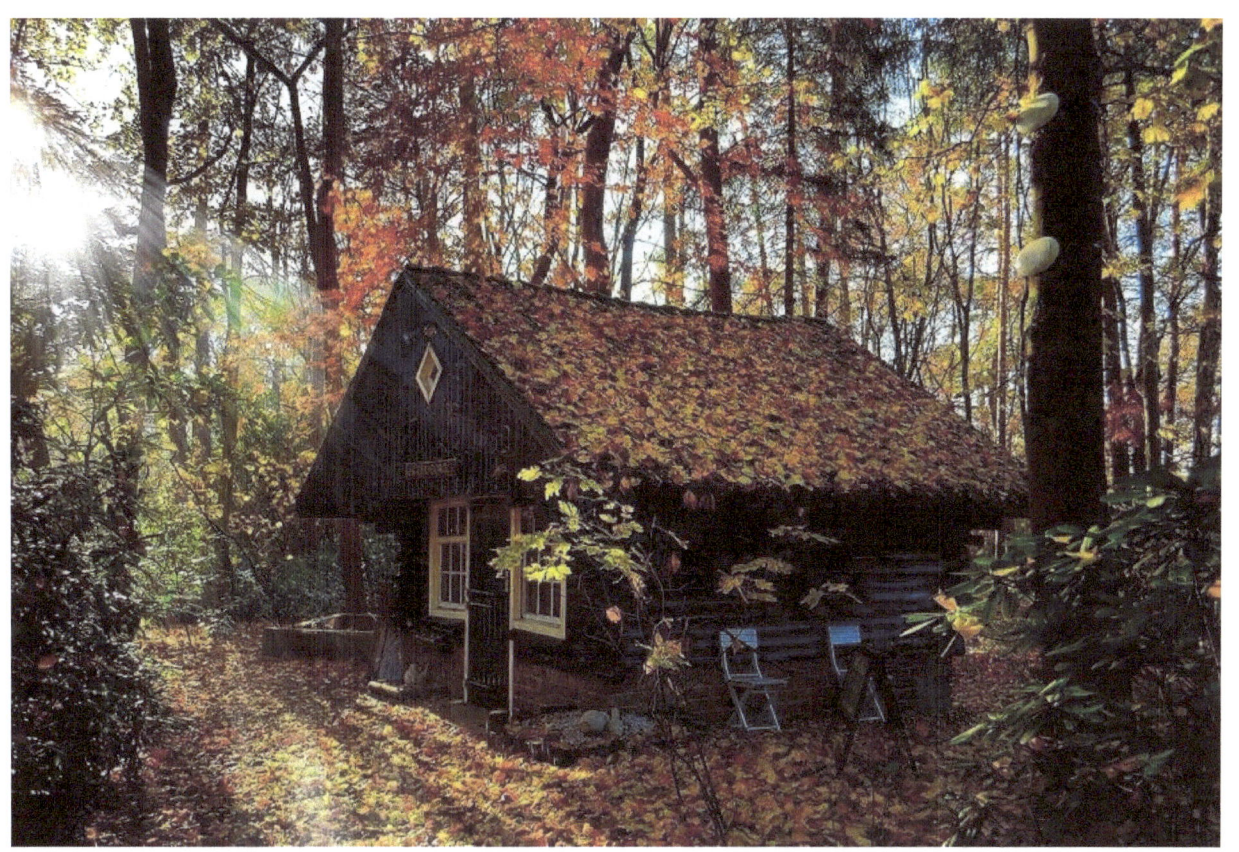

Mother Nature- Maine

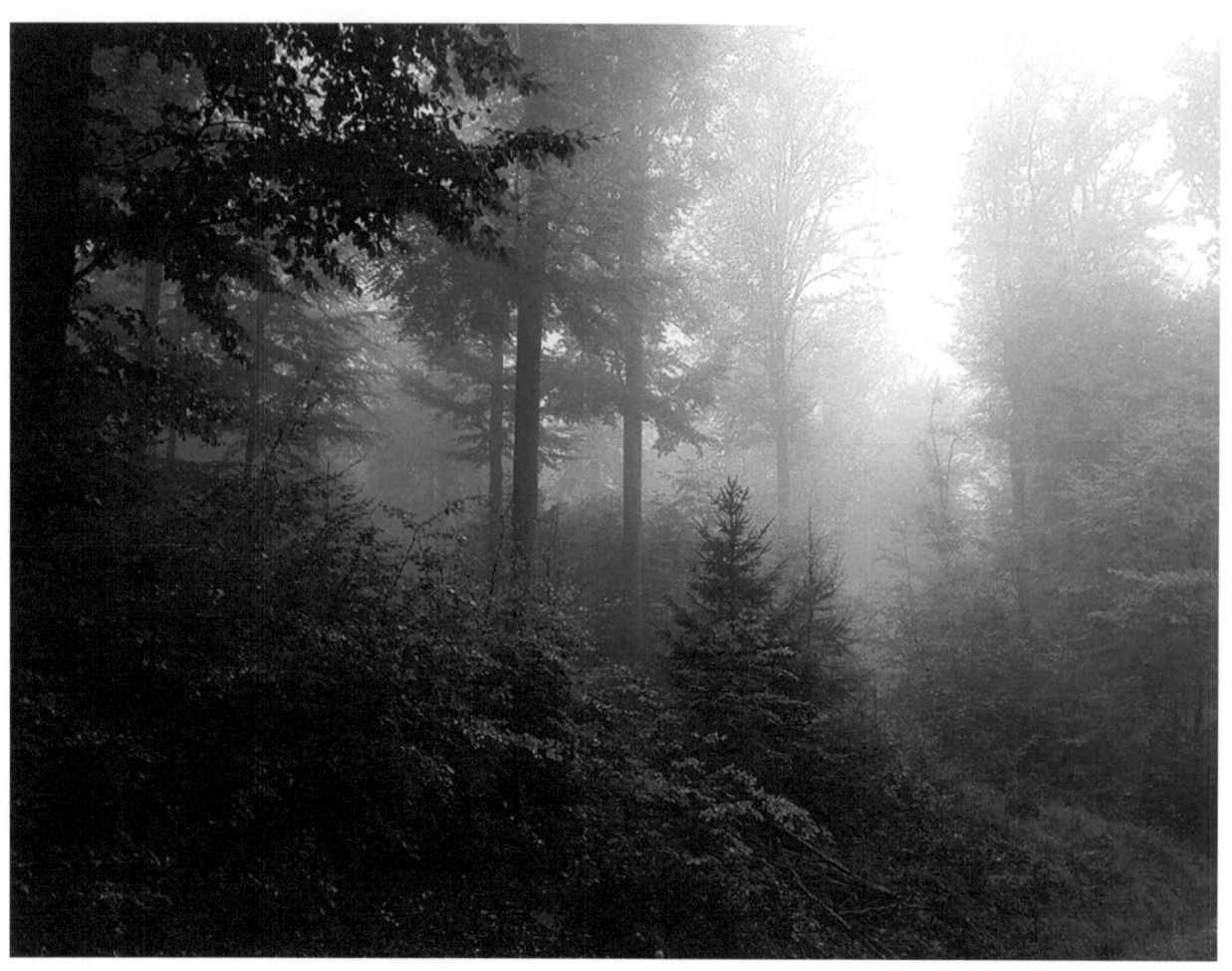

Life- East Hampton New York

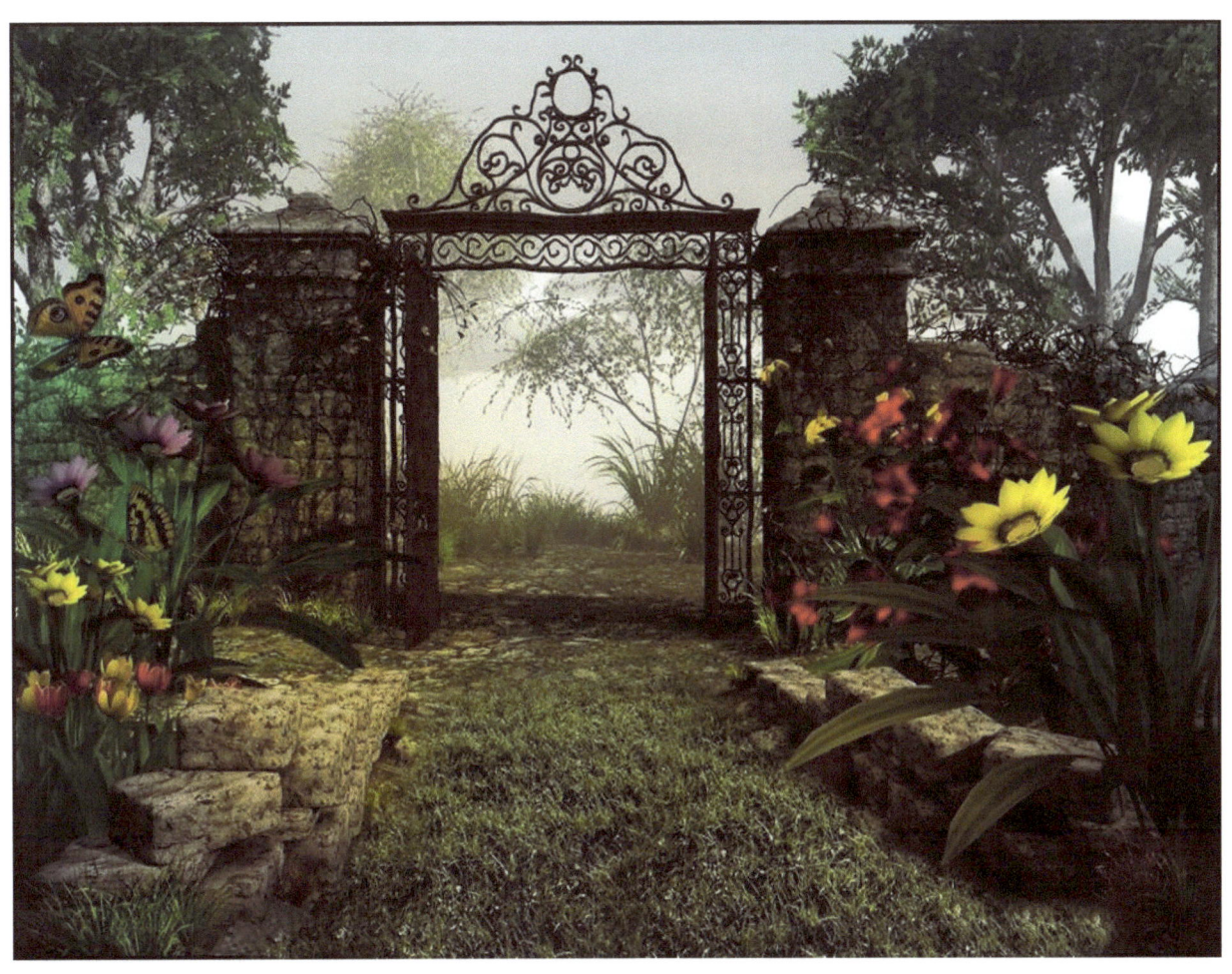

Heavenly Gates- Florida

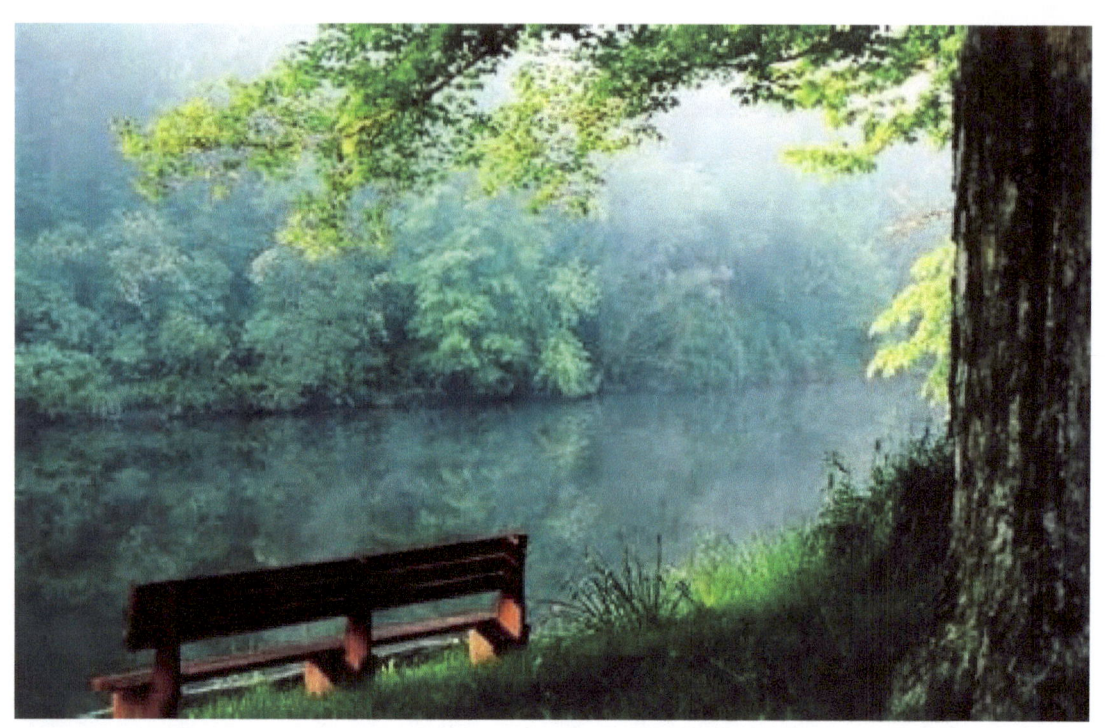

Solace – Central Park, New York

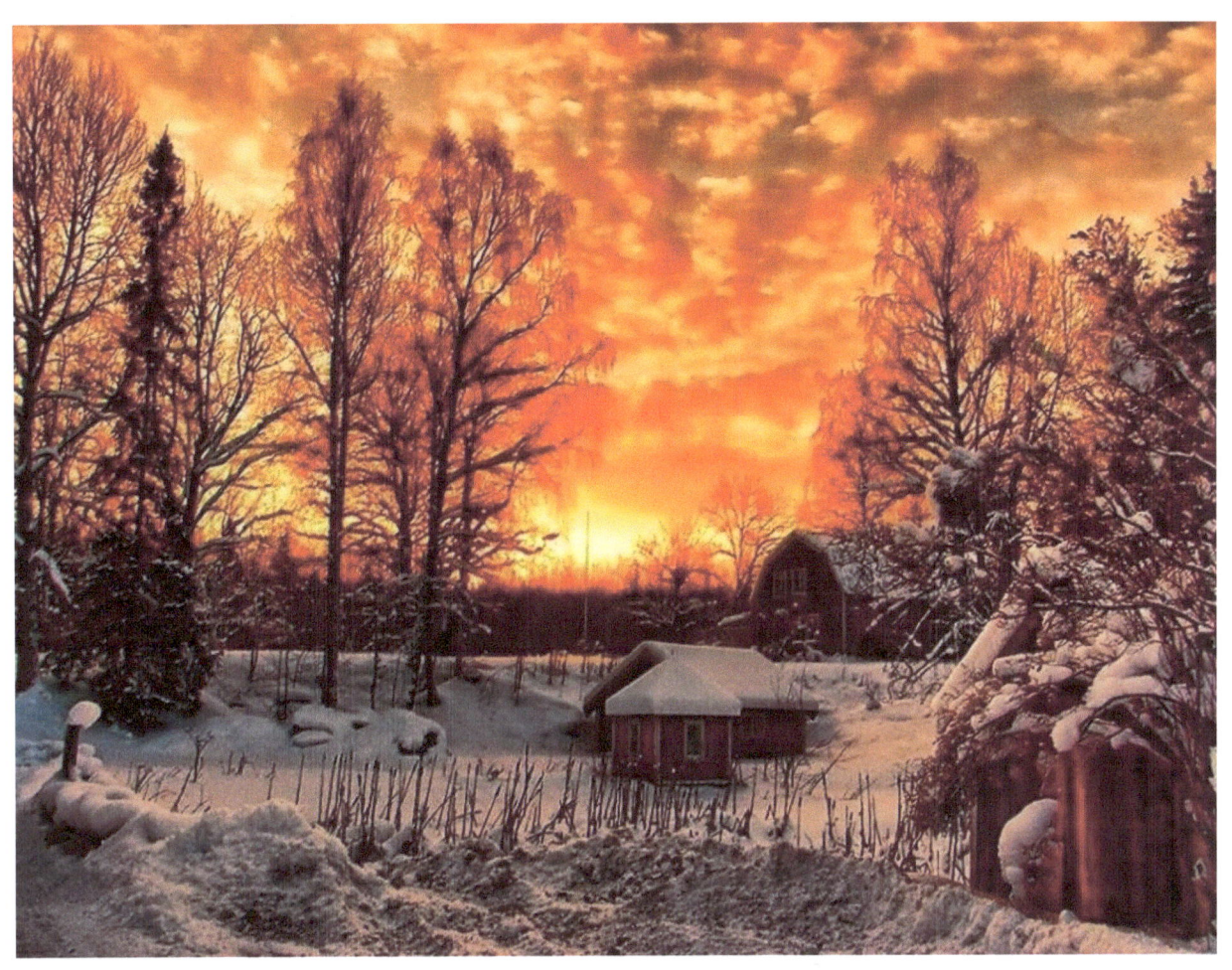

Sky on Fire- Louisville, Kentucky

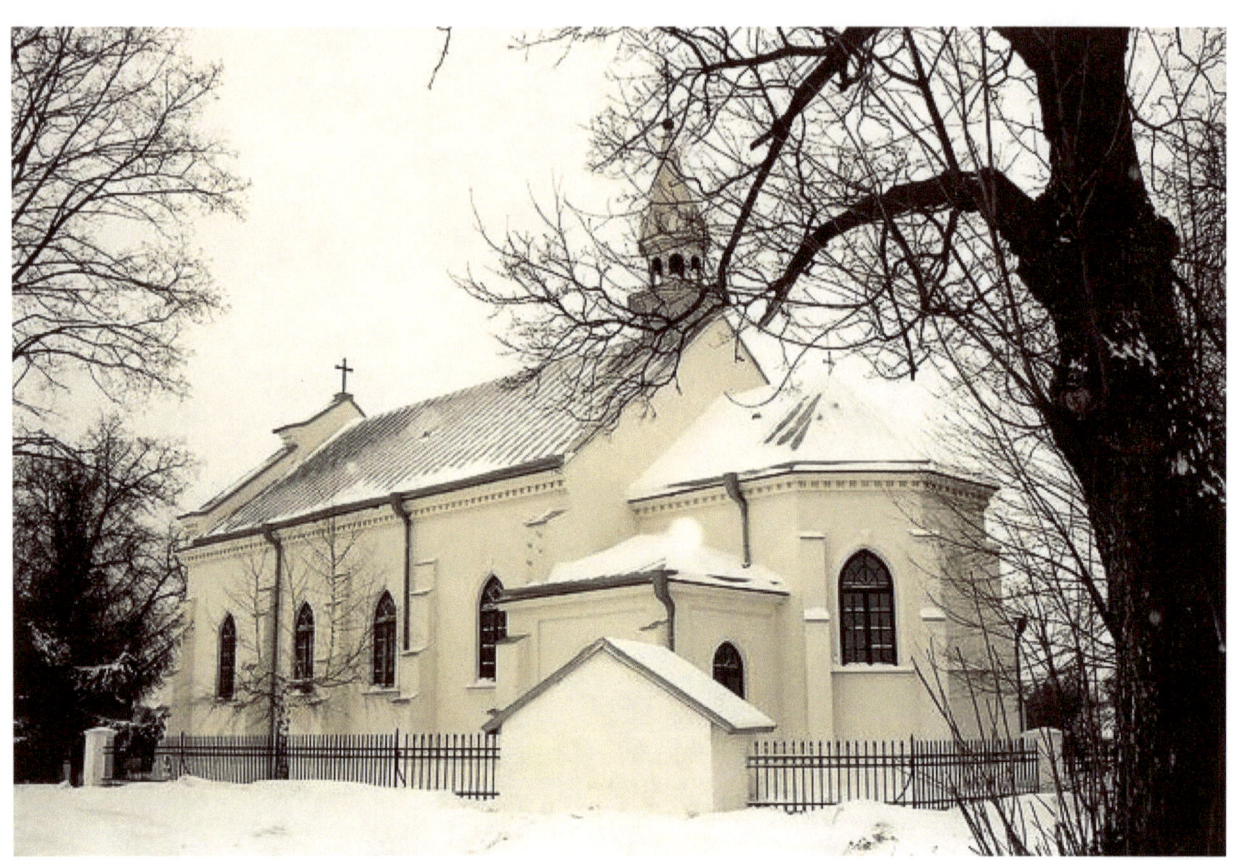

Welcome- P.A.

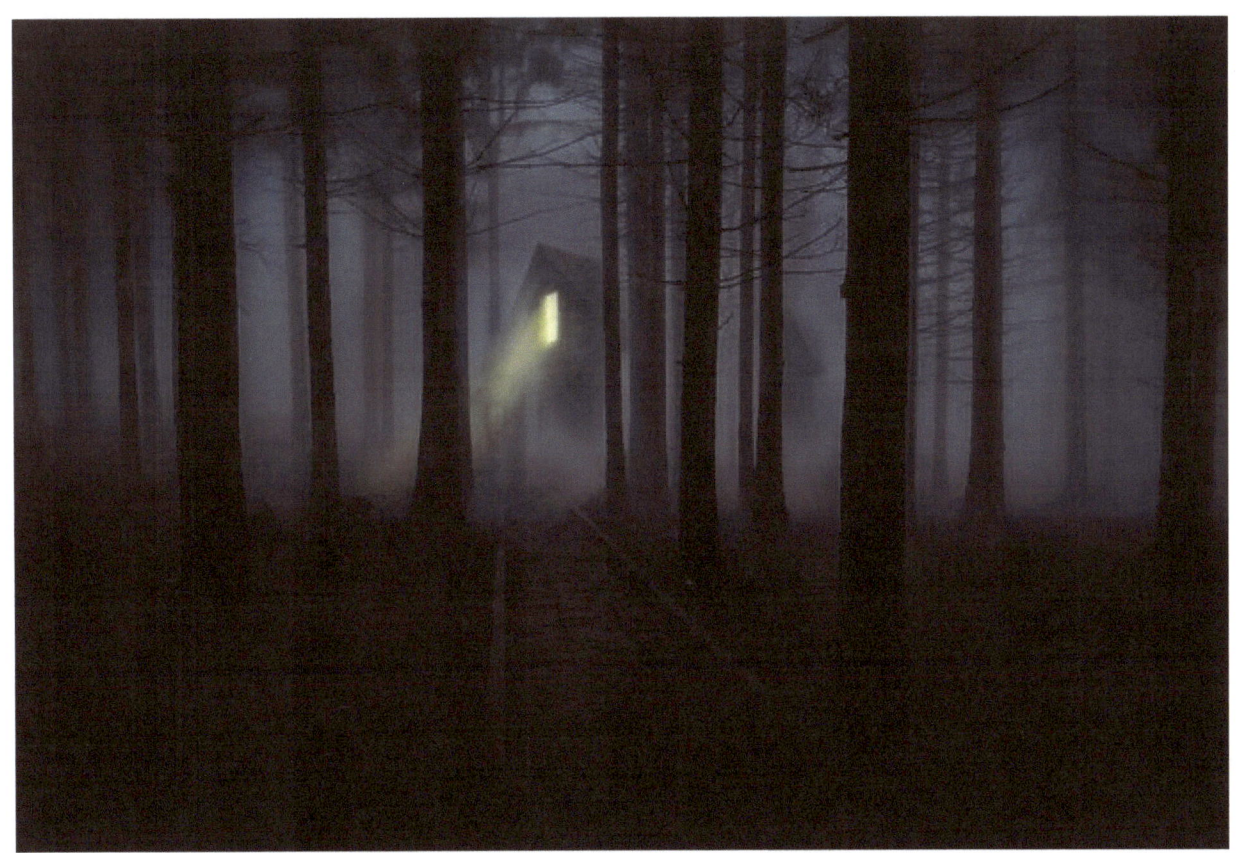

Dark Night- Calf.

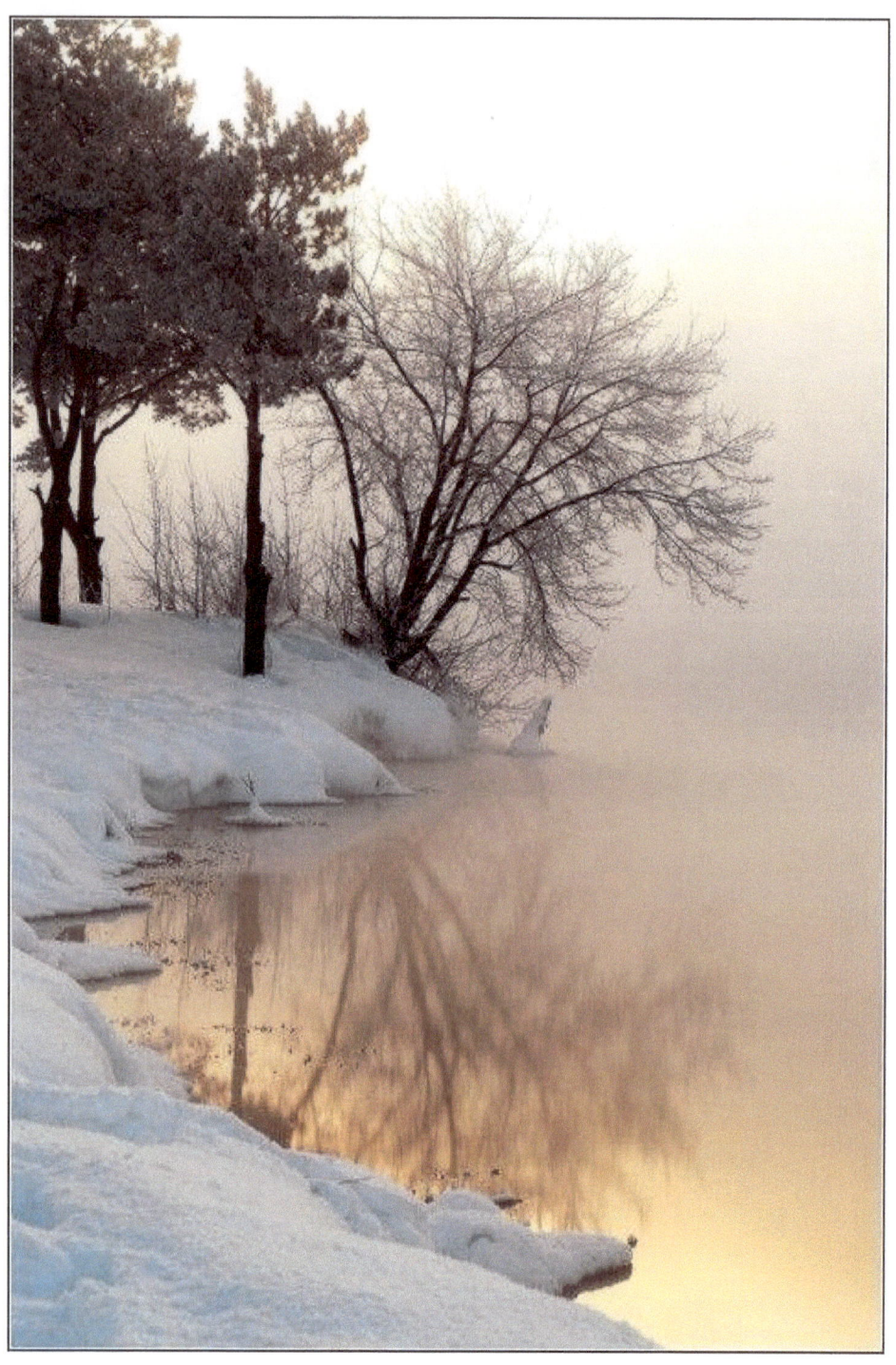

Frozen in Time- Switzerland